One In A Billion

God Leads Us All the Way

by

Lei Deng Cantrell

Bloomington, IN   Milton Keynes, UK

AuthorHouse™
1663 Liberty Drive, Suite 200
Bloomington, IN 47403
www.authorhouse.com
Phone: 1-800-839-8640

AuthorHouse™ UK Ltd.
500 Avebury Boulevard
Central Milton Keynes, MK9 2BE
www.authorhouse.co.uk
Phone: 08001974150

© 2007 Lei Deng Cantrell. All rights reserved.

No part of this book may be reproduced, stored in a retrieval system, or transmitted by any means without the written permission of the author.

First published by AuthorHouse   1/11/2007

ISBN: 978-1-4259-8528-8 (sc)

Printed in the United States of America
Bloomington, Indiana

This book is printed on acid-free paper.

All Scripture references are King James Version, unless indicated NIV.

Scripture taken from the HOLY BIBLE, NEW INTERNATIONAL VERSION®. Copyright © 1973, 1978, 1984 by International Bible Society. Used by permission of Zondervan Publishing House. All rights reserved.

The "NIV" and "New International Version" trademarks are registered in the United States Patent and Trademark Office by International Bible Society. Use of either trademark requires the permission of International Bible Society.

Introduction

I want to dedicate this book to my Savior Jesus Christ, the Lord God Almighty. I praise and thank him. He brought me here and gave me the opportunity to know and follow him, and to learn to do his will. He has enriched my life and I am growing spiritually mature. I am grateful for his mercy and love.

I have been living in Springfield, Missouri since 1993. Because I am Chinese, people ask me questions. They want to know how I came to this country, studied, worked, and lived. Why did I come to Springfield and Evangel College? Was it difficult for me to get out of China to come to America? Why am I not a Buddist, since I am Chinese, and how did I become a Christian? Why do I work at Old Country Buffet? Why don't I get a better job since I have an AA degree in Mental Health Psychology? And so on. I have been answering these same questions thousands of times. I know there will be more to come, so I decided to write down my experiences in a book. I hope and pray I can satisfy everyones' curiosity.

I would like to mention my parents, who spent most of their savings to buy my plane tickets to come over to study. They gave me my early years of training and a good foundation. I give them thanks and honor. I want to give thanks to my husband and daughter, who stand by me and support me. To Margaret Chow, a missionary from China to South America, I am grateful for her wise advise through the years. To my dearest friend and spiritual counselor Rev. Dwight Colbaugh, whom I seek for help in almost everything: I thank you for your understanding and counsel, which has equipped my growth, and for being my close friend and surrogate father. I couldn't have made it this far without you. To Dr. Pansy Collins, my English supervisor, who understood my culture, I gave you thanks for your advise. To my manager Sissy Kahl, an open-minded lady at Old Country Buffet, who I worked with for seven years. She has coached and tolerated me through all these years. For her leadership and entrusting me with my work, teaching me to be patient with my co-workers, and how to be a supervisor based on her experiences: I thank you for your support. I want to show my appreciation to my friend Shelly Lewis, who allowed me to share our story in the book. For my church, I thank Charles Nickel for his guidance and direction to discipline my daughter in a Christian way. I appreciate your work.

Also, this book is in memory of Dr. June Kean, former organist and teacher from Evangel University, who was used by God to be my sponsor. Without her I wouldn't be here to tell my story. For Dr. Donald Bussmann, a great physician. He and his family helped me during my school years. And Rev. Frank Nickel, long time pastor of Southern Heights Bible Church, who went to be with the Lord in November, 2002. Pastor Nickel was able to meet my parents when they came to visit just before he was seriously ill. I give tribute to these people. Their memories I will certainly share with you. I miss them greatly.

Foreword

The truth is, God is involved in our lives, even before we know him. Bringing Lei into my life is one of the greatest things he has done for me. And that is why we are here, to glorify God for what he has done and to bear witness of him, that he will do the same for you, according to his love and great purpose.

In Jesus' Name,

Tim Cantrell

Chapter One

Meeting Dr. June Kean

I first met Dr. June Kean December, 1992, in Beijing, China. At the time I was studying English at night school. I had been interested in foreign languages for a long time, and I dreamed to come to America to study English. But, my family could not support me. It was close to Christmas (At that time, I just knew it was Jesus' birthday, who was a Savior for the foreign world). My parents were working hard to get their church choir ready for Christmas performances. My dad asked me to go to meet Dr. Kean to practice my English with her. She was an organist from America, and came to Central Music Conservatory, where my mom works, to do some teaching and cultural exchange. She agreed to help my mom to accompany her choir on the organ. So I got enough courage and went to Beijing Music Concert Hall, where they were practicing.

When I got there, I saw a woman sitting on the cold staircase talking with some choir members. I tried my best to understand her heavy American accent. Now I know it is "Ozark" English. She wore very heavy make-up and lipstick. It seemed that she never combed or brushed her hair. My jaw dropped when I saw her big feet. She was heavy set and that made her ankles swollen. She carried a purse with her everywhere, but she could not find the things she needed from there. Her questions were so funny to me back then. I understand now it is called "culture shock". She asked why Chinese people worked on holidays such as Christmas and New Year's eve. I told her that was because we are not selfish and we love our neighbors, so we support each other. Why do we only allow one child per family? My reply was, "We are overpopulated."

Soon I found out that she has a strange personality and was very opinionated. My parents invited her to a nice restaurant to have dinner, but she refused and told us that she liked a place and wanted us to go with her to save my parents some money. I thought this woman must have problems in her mind. To my amazement, in a short month, she had learned about more places and how to get there, than people who had lived there all their lives. I began to look at her differently.

Just a few days before the Christmas performance, she found out that I was studying English. So she wrote down my name and address. But it never entered into my mind that she was really going to help me. And I didn't have any idea that meeting her, and getting to know her, was God's will for me to change my life. Praise His Holy Name.

After Christmas, Dr. Kean went home. We didn't hear from her for three months. So I thought she was just like other foreigners that I practiced English with. I went on with my life. But then, we received a letter. Because of the passing of her mother, she had not contacted us. She went through a grieving time, and was going to talk to the school's English Department. My heart pumped hard with excitement, and the hope was burning within me. I thought finally my dream was going to come true through this kind lady.

Then, the waiting began. My parents tried to comfort me by telling me not to worry. A month later, we received another letter, stating that Dr. Kean has talked to the head of the English Department, and Enrollment Office, and they were sending forms to me. Weeks of waiting made me feel like my black hair would turn gray. Finally, the Foreign Student and Enrollment forms came. I began the process of my passport and visa application. I want you to pay attention to the work of God and his humor here.

In order to apply for the passport, I must get the forms officially translated. And we jumped for joy after we saw the translation on the expensive four-year tuition that the school would pay for. My parents thought that was a miracle for my family, and all they thought had to be done was to scrape the money together to buy the plane tickets.

Some people ask me if it was difficult to get a passport out of China? No, the difficult part was to get a visa from the US Embassy.

After I received my passport, I gathered all the papers to apply for a visa. That was a day I will never forget. I got up early in the morning, and rode my bike to the American Embassy. I didn't know what to expect. It was before eight o'clock and there was already a long line. I had to pick a number and wait. Pretty soon the sun shone on the street and it was the middle of July. I paced back and forth, and there were only two voices in my head -- "grant it," and "denied." Finally, after three hours of waiting, it was my turn to go in.

Inside the room, there were bunches of people waiting. And there were three windows. Two small windows by the wall and a big one in the middle. The one on the left was to get a visa for official duties, the one on the right was for students and people with personal matters. And the one sitting behind the big window was the American officer who decides your destiny. I waited in line to hand all the required paperwork into the small window on the right. While I was in line, I saw a woman was questioned by the officer. The woman insisted her answer to the officer was to visit her uncle. But she couldn't get a pass, and her persistence only made the officer extremely angry, and he said, "Lady, look behind you, there are hundreds of people waiting. **Get Out!**" Those were his exact words.

Having been nervous all morning, I had sweated terribly, and after witnessing this horrible scene, I began to tremble. I was told to sit down and wait for that officer to call me. Another long wait. I was so scared I didn't hear the officer call my name. After realizing I had been called, I went to stand in front of the big window and tried not to shake too much. I was questioned why I wanted to go to America? How did I know the school and how did I find Dr. Kean as my sponsor? The officer found my answers quite amusing and he joked and laughed. I believed he had seen my pale face, so maybe he tried to make me at ease. But I kept my face straight, because I didn't know what was going to happen. After all the questions, he picked out a piece of yellow paper, and wrote some numbers on it, handed it to me and said, "Come back in two weeks to pick up your visa."

I walked out the door like a robot, and was in a daze. I got home at three o'clock in the afternoon. My mom told me that my grandma had called and asked me to call back.

I called her and her voice was anxious. She had been shocked by something. She told me that at 5 am while she was still in bed, there were two magpies standing in the tree in front of her apartment, singing out loud towards her bedroom window for thirty minutes. Let me explain: For Chinese, the magpie is a kind of bird that is rarely seen. They represent good news and prosperity, so when one sees a magpie, it means good fortune, happiness or good news are to come to this person or their family. You can understand why my grandma was excited by seeing two magpies at the same time. I told her the good news, and she was happy. My family celebrated and prepared for my departure.

At 6:00 am on Thursday, August 19th, 1993, my family hugged me at the airport before I got on the plane. Then I set out to an adventure which I would've never imagined.

Chapter Two

The Culture Shock
and
My first Semester

I left China Thursday morning, August 19th, 1993. My plane was delayed at Denver, because of weather. I arrived in Springfield, Mo. late that same night. Dr. Kean and another Chinese girl she had sponsored were waiting for me. My belongings were two suitcases, one travel bag, and a purse. We took a ride to her house.

On the way, she gave us a little tour. I could not believe how quiet it was on the street. There were not many pedestrians on the sidewalk. She explained it was dangerous walking at night. I couldn't quite understand it then. Except for cars, there wasn't much traffic, and few people riding bikes. In Beijing, bicycles have been our main transportation, just like driving cars here. We also have a license to ride bicycles. I was surprised to see few city buses with few passengers on them. Not until I started working at Old Country Buffet did I realize that big buses are for tour groups and the city buses are for those people who can't afford vehicles. In China, at night, it would be crowded: People would be sitting outside their houses chatting, playing games with neighbors, and enjoying the moonlight. At times they would move their bed outside to rest and smell the cool night air. Please note: Beijing and Springfield are on the same latitude, so our weather is pretty much the same, only Springfield's weather changes more dramatically than Beijing. It took me two years to adjust.

At Dr. Kean's house, we did nothing but sleep for three days. Then, she took us to Evangel College (now University), and settled us in different dormitories. I was at Burgess Hall.

My first roommate Karen treated me kindly and with great patience. I liked her a lot. She showed me the dorm and introduced me to her friends. She showed me how to use money and how to shop at Walmart. I had to buy a blanket and a pillow, since I didn't bring any. Karen found it interesting that I slept during the day and stayed awake till 4am in the morning, because of the fourteen hours time difference between Beijing and Springfield. It took me three weeks to get over that.

My roommate corrected my English in kind ways. Jan was our suitemate, my roommate's best friend. I made a mistake by telling her that her chubby feet looked so cute. I learned a lesson after that. Jan also helped me to open up an account at the Commerce Bank close by. She taught me how to use the checkbook. I thought it was so interesting to write checks instead of using cash.

My first American food at the school cafeteria was a hamburger. I never had a hamburger in my life until that day. We do have McDonald's in Beijing, but I had never been there. Anyway, I couldn't swallow the hamburger, even though I was so hungry, so I tried all the soft drinks, coffee and tea there to help me to eat that thing. It didn't work. Finally, hot water did. I have a stomach problem and I cannot drink anything cold. If I drink or eat anything that is not warm or hot, it would send me to the toilet for half an hour. So, that is why I have been drinking hot water since then. During the first week of September, I craved Chinese food terribly. My new friends took me to Happy Family Chinese restaurant. At first I was excited. Then after I saw and tasted the food, I tried hard not to cry. The Chinese food here has been Americanized -- it concentrates on sweet and sour and spicy. And some Chinese restaurant's owners are from Vietnam or other Asian countries. They open up the business just to attract Americans. I became homesick. But I thought if I want to stay for four years, I'd better learn to eat American food. So I tried a little bit at a time. After two years, I finally felt comfortable with the food, and was able to enjoy it like my own.

The biggest challenge for me was language. Even though I have been learning English since I was 12 years old, when I had my first class, I knew I had a long way to go. Fortunately, I brought a tape recorder and two English-Chinese dictionaries from home. So every day I took my books and tape recorder to each of my classes, and I jotted down whatever I could understand during the class hour. After supper, I would play the tapes over and over to make sure I had not missed anything, and I looked up the words and phrases. At the end of the semester, I was able to pass the final exams of my classes. It was not easy.

I was majoring in English. Besides taking English classes, I had to have Bible and other general education classes to make up my credits.

My first Bible class was "The Gospel of John." Mr. Nell Fry was my Bible teacher. He was a big man and very tall. He was a missionary. On the first day of the class when he found out I came from China, he gave me a big bow, and it scared me so much that I almost jumped out of my chair. As a student in China, you are supposed to bow to your teacher, and stand up to answer questions unless the teacher tells you otherwise. This shows you respect the teachers and that you have good discipline. Mr. Fry's teaching made the biblical characters come alive and scripture reading interesting. Even though those long and weird names gave me such a headache, I was drawn to it when the Bible talked about Jesus, how he walked on the water, calmed the storm, fed the hungry people with little food, and his death and resurrection.

Let me stop for a minute, just to make your curiousity go away. No, I didn't get to know Jesus by that time, but it did make me like him a lot. All I tried to do during that first semester was to get my language barrier under control, so I didn't have to bring the dictionaries and tape recorder every time I went to class to get passing grades. Oh well, please don't get disappointed, I do have a little good news to tell you. I got a "C" on my final exam after all the hard work I had done, and without any Bible knowledge. That was a big accomplishment for me for the first time, even Mr. Fry congratulated me. He was so proud of me. He understood how hard it was for me.

Dr. Kean took me out occasionally, just to make sure I was doing well. One day, she took me to Hong Kong Inn, a Chinese restaurant not too far from school. I liked the food and for the next 3 1/2 years, I would walk to Hong Kong Inn on Sundays, just for a change from the school's cafeteria.

One fine Sunday in September, Dr. Kean took me to St. Agnes Church and introduced me to Dr. Donald Bussmann. After we were introduced, I felt comfortable with him right away, because he was a surgeon just like my dad. His wife is a pediatrician and they have three children. Dr. Bussmann was a funny, curious and active person, and he wanted to know everything about me and my country. He was a spirit-filled Catholic, and was faithful to his church and his family. Every Sunday he would come to pick me up from school and take me to church, and bring me back. Every time when he was ready to leave, he would say to me, "Peace be with you, Lei." He bought me an English-Chinese Bible and signed his name and date on the inside cover. I have treasured that Bible. He was always enthusiastic about

God and encouraged me to love him because his Son died for my sin. But I felt empty when I was at Church, because of the old-fashioned Mass and ceremonial kneeling. Except for the Lord's prayer at the end of the service, I couldn't get anything out of the Mass.

Meanwhile, when I was at school, I had to attend the chapel services Monday through Friday. I couldn't catch what those preachers were talking about. It made matters worse when the fellow students asked me the question, "Why attend school if you are not a Christian?" I thought mainly I was having difficulty understanding the language. I didn't tell Dr. Bussmann how I felt. But I was curious about Jesus. When I spent my first Chrismas at my cousin's house in New Jersey, she asked a question, and I didn't know how to answer her. She said, "Jesus died and was buried, but what is so important about that cross? What does that cross have to do with His death and burial?" What I had learned in my Gospel of John class was not enough to satisfy her needs. I sensed an urgency to study the Bible. So I read the Bible from the beginning to the end during Chrismas break at my cousin's house. And I didn't get anything out of that. I was frustrated.

Chapter Three

Life Changing Events
and
"Once I was Blind, Now I See"

I had bad habits. I was (and still am) so proud to be Chinese with such an excellent culture and history. So my nose was in the air. I liked to talk loudly and would easily get angry. I didn't mind anyone. Karen did her best to try to teach me to be humble and act like a lady. But I failed her. We had many talks, but I never took it into my heart. Finally, she gave up and asked me to move out. I moved to the room down the hall and stayed by myself. I was hurt and angry at first. It took me a little while to realize that she was right, and I must change my way of thinking and doing. I adopted American culture for my roommate's sake, and I have no regrets.

By the 1994 Spring semester, my English had improved. I didn't have to take my tape recorder to all of my classes. So I was happy.

Dr. Kean and Dr. Bussmann were quite proud of my progress.

Evangel has Spiritual Emphasis at the beginning of the semester. During that week on Wednesday night, some of my friends asked me to go with them to the chapel. I decided to challenge myself on how much I could understand the preacher. Mr. Jessie Owens was the speaker. He was quite delighted to visit with me.

But my attention was drawn to a very scholar-like figure on the platform with such a beautiful singing voice. Dwight Colbaugh was the Campus Pastor. He married the most beautiful woman in the world and they have three gorgeous daughters. For some reason I felt that I could trust him and talk to him freely. I could understand him easily, also. He asked whether I would like to know Jesus and receive him. I said I would like to try. I sat with him that night and talked and talked. We became good friends. Thursday morning when I went to chapel again, I felt as though my whole being wanted to shout and praise, even though I didn't know why and what to say. Pastor Colbaugh said that he saw the glorious light shine on my face.

Early Friday morning, while I was still asleep, I had a dream. I dreamed I saw a wall in front of my path. On the wall was the word "Seek".   So in the dream I remember telling people around me that I saw the word "Seek". But those people said they didn't see "Seek." Instead they saw "sick." Friday morning when I woke up, I couldn't get out of bed, so I missed chapel service. But, I did go to chapel at the end of service to see Pastor Colbaugh and tell him what I had dreamed. He was excited and said, "It is very interesting, let me pray for you." His prayer was:"Jesus, Lei has found you, she is excited to know more about you. Please show her the meaning of this dream. In Jesus name, Amen!" At that moment I could not control my tears, I was laughing and crying at the same time. I couldn't bring myself to understand what had happened to me. I have always been called strong in my family and seldom cry, but on that day I lost it completely. Pastor Colbaugh said it is OK to cry, because I have renewed myself in Jesus. I didn't quite understand what he meant.

   So during the following week, I went to visit my pastor in his office. I asked him about the meaning of my dream.   His explanation was, "Jesus loved me and asked me to seek him." Growing up, I have always believed there is a God. Remember in chapter one I mentioned that I only knew Jesus was a Saviour for the foreign world. Never did I know that He is **my** Saviour and died for **my** sin too until that day. **How Exciting**! Pastor Colbaugh also said that I could visit his office anytime if I have any questions. He said it in the polite way, but I took it seriously. Did I have any questions? Of course I did! I was like a newborn baby wanting to learn everything. I visited his office so often that I believe his secretary must have wanted to build a thick wall around the chapel so that I wouldn't be able to find the door to get in. But I am here to thank her for her patience with me and allowing me to seek the knowledge of God. Thank you Mrs. Warner.

The first semester, I had to go to chapel services for the sake of attendance. But since February, 1994, after I found Jesus, I got so hungry and thirsty for the Lord that I was eager to go to chapel services. And I found myself beginning to enjoy the sermons, and to understand what the Scriptures meant. It was just like someone had opened my eyes. I saw the Light! I understood that Jesus is the Son of God, became flesh, and was crucified and died on the cross for my sin. His resurrection and Second Coming gives us hope. I am saved by his shed blood, so that I could have

Eternal Life. The verse in the song "Amazing Grace,""Once I was blind, but now I see" fits my situation perfectly.

And most importantly, I realized that Jesus is not just a Saviour for the foreign world, but **he is the Saviour for ALL who want to know him and receive him.** I told Dr. Kean what I had found. She was extremely happy for me. I talked to Dr. Bussmann once in a while on the phone and he did come to school to visit me a few times. The last time I saw him was on my Wedding Day, December 21, 1996, and I didn't go back to St. Agnes Church any more until the visitation of his passing several years later. As for Karen, she graduated in May of 1994, and married at the end of that year. I got a new roommate whose name was Valarie. Her parents were missionaries to Malaysia and we got along very well.

Chapter Four

My Growth in the Lord During School

So when I became a new believer, my Father in Heaven gave me his love, protection, taught me of his words, and disciplined me when I made mistakes. He answered my prayers, and he forgave me when I repented. In this chapter, I would like to share how the Lord drew me closer to him, step by step, and about his discipline to me during my school years.

Remember when I was preparing to come over to the USA, my parents thought it was a miracle that my four years tuition would be paid by the school. Well, it turned out to be a huge mistake. Two weeks after I arrived at school, I received the bill. I was in shock and depressed. My parents were so angry, but couldn't do anything to help me. Let me explain: Chinese currency is called RMB Yuan. Eight Yuan is equivalent to one American Dollar. Ten years ago, both my parents' salaries combined to three hundred Yuan, or less than fourty dollars a month. So there was no way I would ask them to help me, even though they wholeheartedly wanted to. But after negotiation, the school agreed to pay for the first year, and the final three years I would be on my own. So in October of 1993, I started working at the school cafeteria as a line server and dish washer. I had to get a Social Security Card, and go to the Immigration Department in Kansas City to get a permit to work on campus. With a paycheck every two weeks, I was able to get by. But I spent most of that money calling home for a whole year, and didn't save much.

By the end of Spring semester 1994, I felt hopeless to continue my schooling. I was worried. So on a rainy Monday morning at 11am, just two weeks before the spring semester would end, I called Pastor Colbaugh to pray for me. After that, I prayed a bold prayer. My prayer was, "Heavenly Father, I know you are the Powerful God, and you know what I need. If there is any hope for me to continue my schooling, please stop the rain. In Jesus name, Amen!" After I prayed, I took my umbrella and books to go to class. As I walked to the class with my umbrella open, I noticed the rain has stopped and the sunshine appeared in the sky. It was just five minutes and then rained again. But five minutes was enough for me to regain my hope and trust in him. I cried out, "Praise the Lord." I knew he had heard my prayer and provided the Sign for me to show his love and care for me. You may think that was just a coincidence and doesn't mean anything. Well, think whatever you like. The Lord knows the heart of his children and what he provided that morning drew me closer to him and strengthened my faith as a new believer to grow in him. Praise his Holy Name!

Summer vacation started and I was invited by the Richard Lawson family to Arkansas. Rick told me I could work in the factory for tuition during those four months. I went to the Immigration office again and got a permit to work outside the campus. Then at the end of May, I started working. I worked on the assembly line by picking up the machine-made lawn chairs. I started with the small ones. They were hot after they dropped down from the machine and I was to pick them up and set them on the stool to cool off. Then I put them on the table to use a special knife to trim the edges of the chair until it felt smooth. And then I would put four rubber plugs into the bottom of the chair legs, so that when I pulled the chair on the floor, it wouldn't make a squeaky sound. For a month, I stood on my feet from five-in-the-afternoon to seven-in-the-morning, with two 30-minute breaks. And talk about hardship, I am proud to say I experienced it. Picture this girl from a big city, having never worked a 14-hour shift before. Every morning, I walked like a ninety-year-old woman in need of a cane. Otherwise, I would have fallen down. The only nice thing about this job was the good pay: I mailed about a thousand dollars back to school in a month. I thought everything went well until I injured my thumb and related muscles while I was working. I went from the fastest to the slowest: I was fired. Then I worked for a company that assembled air conditioning parts for the rest of the summer. I went to church with Rick on Sundays, and only then was I able to rest in the Lord, and knew he was with me during the difficult times while I was on my feet and cried in my heart. Thanks be to God!

During the time while I worked my second job, my host family played a role of matchmaking. A young man from China attending school in Nashville, Tennessee came down to work as a door-to-door salesman. I will just call him Young. So my host family thought it would be nice for us to be together. But I always worked, so we talked on the phone.

Coming back to school, my English had gotten much better after I learned all the Arkansas English. I didn't have to take my tape recorder to classes any more, and that made Dr. Kean and Dr. Bussmann really happy. I continued my schooling as the Lord had promised and worked for the school Security office during winter vacation. I stayed with Sherry Blanchard's family and visited their church. And I continued my conversation with Young on the phone.

The year of 1995 was a transition for me to know God, who truly is a Healer, Deliverer, and disciplines in his way.

Pastor Colbaugh has been a father-figure to me. His disciplinary method reminds me of God's love to his children -- gentle and meaningful. One day, I went by the Chapel office, and I noticed that Mrs. Warner, the secretary, had a nice hair-do. I complimented her. Jerry was the Chapel sound technician. He heard my compliment and began to pay attention to Mrs. Warner's hair. With a full pride, I hit Jerry with my hip. From my point of view, what I did was not a big deal, because I have watched it on TV. Pastor Colbaugh caught me right on the spot. He smiled widely and said, "Lei was a good girl, but she learned bad things since she came over here." There was no harsh language, but a gentle touch on my head. The scriptures have spoken, **"For they verily for a few days chastened us after their own pleasure; but he for our profit, that we might be partakers of his holiness" (Hebrew 12:10). "But when we are judged, we are chastened of the Lord, that we should not be condemned with the world" (1 Corinthians 11:32).** Thanks to Pastor Colbaugh for his godly council, I learned a valuable lesson.

In the Spring of 1995, I had a sharp pain in my chest for almost a week. It was hard for me to breath. I guess it was stress related, and I was scared. I had no insurance. The pain started on Monday and continued through Thursday. That night while I was asleep, I had a dream. I dreamed I was sitting on the couch watching TV and a man came to sit down next to me. He didn't wear a shirt. And he asked how I was doing. I told him how I felt and about my problems. After I finished talking, he asked me to look at him, and said, "Look, I didn't do anything wrong, but they whipped my back and pierced my side." He turned around to show me the scars on his back, and asked me to feel his wound on his side with my finger. I felt it. The wound was still soft. And then he said, "Compared to what I was going through, he bore much more than I can imagine." Having said that, he reached out his hand and touched me. I felt heat go through me. I didn't know what to think so I hid my face between my knees. When I looked up again, he was nowhere to be found.

Friday morning I went to attend chapel service as usual. It happened to be Dr. Spence, the school President, preaching. When he stated, "Jesus went to a mountain to pray," I took a deep breath, and noticed my chest pain was gone and I could breath easily. After the service, I went to see my pastor right away and shared my experience with him. And we both believed that Lord Jesus himself appeared in my dream and healed me. That was my first time experiencing his healing. Now I believed strongly in his Presence and his love and closeness to his children. Give him thanks and glory. Hallelujah! Praise his Holy Name!

Young finally decided to come to visit me at the end of summer of 1995 after we talked on the phone for a whole year. I was working as a housekeeper at school, and stayed with Jan Schmidt's family. And I visited Oak Grove Assembly with them during my stay.

I met Young just a couple of weeks before school started. I was quite disappointed with Young's looks compared to the picture he sent me. But I liked how he made me laugh when he talked about Chinese jokes. We both had two things in common -- speaking Chinese and being home-sick. We decided to go back to Arkansas to visit my host family. They took us on a canoe trip.

It was my first time in a canoe. It was burning hot and humid. So I laid my life jacket, a shirt and pair of shoes on the canoe floor. When we came to an area where the water was very deep and looked like a whirlpool, we lost control. My boat flipped over and was sucked under the water, and I was under the boat. I have never been a good swimmer and of course I never learned to open my eyes under water. Plus, I am short. While Young and other people were wondering where I was, they saw my life jacket float away. I was struggling to get out. I was not strong enough to push the canoe off of my head. I didn't know how close I came to drowning. I remember when I was struggling, my left foot got hooked on something very hard. As desperate as I was, I pulled it toward me and rode on it, and it gently flowed me out of the water. After my eyes opened, I saw myself riding on a thick branch. Thank God Almighty! After I was helped to shore, I started shaking for a long time. On that day, God saved and delivered me out of danger. I am alive to tell the story today, just to let you know that he is with you everywhere and will deliver you out of trouble.

After that, Young went back to school. We continued talking on the phone.

Then began the Fall semester, 1995. I went to Chapel as usual. It was Dr. Spence's welcoming all of the new students and he told us to greet each other. So I greeted everyone in front of me and behind me and the one on my right. After I sat down, a guy on my left in his mid-thirties greeted me, and introduced himself as Tim Cantrell. He was a freshman. And I welcomed him too.

The Fall of 1995 went by fast, and I wanted to see Young and start a friendship with him, since we are from the same culture. So I prayed day and night for God to show me if Young was the right person for me. Two weeks before Christmas, I decided to trick Young. I told him on the phone that I had bought a plane ticket and was ready to visit him during Christmas. The Lord forgave me for this lie. Young thought I was serious and told me that it was not a good idea, because he wouldn't know where to put me. So before I went to bed that night, I prayed one last time for the Lord to show me whether Young was the right one for me.

In the middle of the night, I had a dream. In the dream I was going to go somewhere. When I was ready to set off, I heard thunder and saw lightning. The lightning was as sharp as a knife dropping down from the sky and cut off the path in front of me. And then I heard this angry and loud voice: <u>*"NO!!!"*</u>. I awakened by the voice from my sleep and found my heart beating fast like a hundred miles an hour. The echo of the voice remained in my ear for a long time. There was no one else but myself in the room. I did not have a roommate at that time. My whole body was surrounded by the tremendous heat. It was not like I have been burned by fire, because I didn't feel any pain. I couldn't explain it in any other way. So in the morning I went to see Pastor Colbaugh in a hurry and told him what had happened to me. He prayed that the Lord would reveal to me the answer.

That night I called Young again, and he told me: "I don't want you to come over. I have a girlfriend already. I like you, but you are not my type. I went to see you during summer to find out whether you were better than my girlfriend. I am sorry I lied to you. I wish you well."

I put down the phone and cried. Afterward I praised God for stopping me before I made a fool of myself. I learned a lesson from that experience. God's timing is perfect. His love for us is sufficient. He is our Heavenly Father and he cares for our well-being and has the best plans for our future. Ask him for guidance and do not lean on your own understanding, and you will be all right. For the Lord has spoken: **"In all your ways acknowledge him, and he will make your paths straight" (Proverbs 3:6, NIV).**

"Whether you turn to the right or to the left, your ears will hear a voice behind you, saying, 'This is the way; walk in it'" (Isaiah 30:21, NIV).

"A man's heart deviseth his way: but the Lord directeth his steps" (Proverbs 16:9).

Praise his Holy Name, for he is just. HalleluYah!

Chapter Five

My Walk with The Lord
and
God's Provision for a Future Mate

I worked in the school cafeteria each semester. And every time I got paid, I would use some of the money to pay phone bills. I learned to cut the cost of calling home so often. I also used some of the money to buy text books. I learned to trade the used books with other students in order to save some money to pay for tuition. Good thing I didn't have to buy groceries, otherwise I would be really broke. Anyway, I couldn't make enough to pay off the tuition, so Evangel decided that I needed to change my degree from Bachelor of Art in English to Associate of Art in Mental Health Psychology. That way I could graduate early in order to save me from having a huge amount of debt. I didn't understand what an AA degree meant, until I found out later it was less than a BA degree. I would graduate in May of 1996 instead of 1997. That was part of the reason for my chest pain, which I mentioned in the last chapter.

I knew I had to concentrate on my studies instead of worrying too much about what my family might think of me and how I had failed Dr. Kean, after she worked so hard to sponsor me. My parents tried to comfort me by telling me they knew I had done my best, and asked me to come back home after graduation.

My heart had changed since the day I received Christ as my Lord and Savior in the Spring of 1994. After I told my family the exciting news, they could not understand what I was talking about. They have no idea what it means to become a new person. I then came to a realization: On the day of my departure to America, I waved good-bye to my parents facing the other way. At that time, I didn't want them to see me cry. But now I knew that not only did I wave good-bye to my parents, but also to my past. I was growing in the Lord and his love is great.

The Spring of 1996 was my last semester at Evangel. I enjoyed answering questions on how I came to Evangel and got saved, and praised the Lord for what he has done for me to fellow students and professors. Pastor Colbaugh called that sharing my testimony. I then found myself praying for other people and telling them that they should come to know the Lord. And Pastor Colbaugh referred to that as witnessing for the Lord. When I changed my major to Mental Health Psychology, I was even more fascinated by how many people are out there in need of God's love.

During the last year at school, I practiced my Psychology and witness at the same time on a girl who became my roommate during Summer School. Lisa came from a complicated background and that made her vulnerable. She lacked confidence. She didn't have much self-esteem and was very insecure. I acted as her counselor and prayed with her. I saw the improvement on how she looked up the Word of God for answers for her life, and forgiveness from her past. We became good friends ever since. Meanwhile, I prayed to see God's plan for my future.

At the Spring semester 1996, I had to do practicum to try out my knowledge on a group of children at Weller Elementary School to complete my credits.

I made an appointment with Mrs. Colbaugh, who was the Principal of Weller, to give me instructions on my practicum. But I didn't know how to get there. After a chapel service,

I was telling Pastor Colbaugh that I might have to cancel the appointment because I did not have a ride. Tim Cantrell was standing by the chapel door and overheard our conversation. He offered to give me a ride. I thought he was so kind. So, I made the trip with his help. After that, I realized that I had to ask for a ride three times a week, for a whole four months. I talked to Tim and he didn't mind. I thanked the Lord for answered prayer and for solving my transportation problem.

So, I worked with behavior-disordered children in one room for an hour, and went to work with mentally-disordered children for another hour. And then I helped the teacher who taught English as a second language. I enjoyed this for a whole semester.

I had visited a few churches on Sundays during school. On Wednesday nights, I would go to the "Mid-week Manna" services in the chapel.

One Wednesday evening in January, 1996, I saw Tim at the school cafeteria and asked him whether there was a service being held in the chapel. He told me there wasn't. I knew Tim was one of the song leaders at chapel service. So while I was ready to go back to my dorm after supper, he asked me if I didn't mind, I could go to visit his church. I was glad to go to church with him.

Southern Heights Bible Church is a small, nondenominational church. A guy wearing a white sweater was leading the Bible Study. He was fairly tall and very chunky. Tim introduced me to everyone. There were not more than ten people there. The chunky guy acted bossy, and was impolite towards an elderly couple sitting in the very front pew, but they just smiled and didn't respond to his rudeness. Everybody talked to me after the service. Paula Clark was very friendly. She made me feel warm and comfortable. The elderly couple asked me to come back to visit again.

On the way back to school, I found out the elderly couple was the Pastor Frank Nickel and his wife Eva. They have eight children. The very chuncky guy was their oldest son Charles, Chuck for short. I questioned why pastor Nickel didn't give the lesson instead of his son. It was because he and his wife were not in good health, so they gave part of their responsibilities to their son. I also learned that Chuck was Principal of Westport Elementary School. That explained his bossiness.

Mrs. Eva Nickel was very happy to see me again when I visited the church the second time a couple weeks later. She wanted to know how I was doing in America. She told me another son and daughter-in-law are missionaries to China, and that made me feel really good.

Pastor Nickel liked to make poems. Paula Clark and other ladies made me feel at ease with this little church. I decided to stay and make it my home church.

The Spring of 1996 was a difficult time for me. First, I was not able to pay off my tuition, and I could not continue school even if I wanted to. What made it worse was that I would be deported if I didn't find a way to turn this situation around. I had asked my bank for student loans, but I couldn't get any, because they weren't sure I could pay them back. Since I am a foreigner, they certainly didn't want to take a risk on me.

I was shocked when Mrs. Sherri Phillips, the Foreign Student Advisor of Evangel asked how my relationship with Tim was going. Tim and I were sort of dating. He was the only one I could ask to give me a ride without having to worry about paying gas money. I became so stingy over money during the time at Evangel. He liked Chinese food and we would eat at Hong Kong Inn. I liked pizza. Tim would take me to Ci'Ci's Pizza for the $2.99 buffet.

Plus, he had taken me to practicum three times a week, rain or shine. I enjoyed his company. Both of us had a great desire to serve the Lord. He has a beautiful voice.

But, one thing made me keep distance from him: He was an unwed father of two girls. From the Chinese point of view, this kind of person deserves to go down to the bottom of the pit. Children born out of wedlock would be picked on for the rest of their lives. I was shocked to find out after I came to America that China has changed dramatically. Young people there have not kept the tradition of a pure dating process. They are allowed to live together without feeling any shame. Oh Lord, what has the world come to?

I called my cousin in New Jersey, and told her what was going on and asked her advise. She is a very open-minded person. She suggested that I should try everything possible to get to know Tim better. And she told me don't let my feelings ruin what is in my heart. So, when Mrs. Phillips asked my relationship with Tim, I told her he was a nice person, and I enjoyed his presence very much, and we had a lot of things in common. And most of all, we have a great desire to serve the Lord together. Then

Mrs. Phillips' advise for me was, "Do whatever is best for you and your future."

I prayed over this. Tim and I talked and talked and talked for ten months. For seven months, I tried everything possible just to get to know him. I asked his relatives, friends, and everyone I could think of to tell me about him. I had never asked that many questions in my life.

Tim seemed very content and had peace about this all this time. He asked me to marry him about eight times, and I turned him down seven. I told him if he wanted to marry me, he must write to my parents in order to get their approval. He did and my parents had a difficult time accepting. They worried about my well-being and how I would handle his past. I don't blame them, and I believe I would do the same for my child.

In May of 1996, I graduated from Evangel with an AA degree in Mental Health Psychology. I moved out of Burgess Hall where I have lived for three years, and into Spence Hall for summer break. I applied to work as a mental health technician at local hospitals and clinics. None of them wanted to train me. I was desperate. My church prayed that the Lord would guide me through this tough time.

In July of 1996, I left Evangel and moved in with a friend of ours. Tim moved in with Pastor Nickel for a few months. Mrs. Nickel had passed away in May of 1996. I finally accepted Tim's proposal in August. Pastor Colbaugh performed pre-marital counselling for us. In September, I applied to work at Old Country Buffet and they hired me. We set our wedding date for Saturday, December 21st, 1996. I worked at Old Country Buffet to save money for my wedding. In October, we sent invitations to everybody we knew to come to our wedding. The Lord was with us.

Chapter Six

The Precious Gift from Heaven
and
God's Faithfulness

My grandmother gave me her blessing on the phone before her passing. I prayed that she rests in the Lord.

Saturday, December 21st, 1996, we married at Southern Heights Bible Church. My parents couldn't come, so Pastor Colbaugh walked me down the isle and performed the ceremony. Dr. Kean played the wedding song for me. Lisa was my bridesmaid. Dr. Bussmann and his wife came to my wedding. Margaret Chow, a missionary from China to South America, came also. The rest were Tim's family and friends. It was a simple, yet formal and meaningful wedding. We went to Arkansas for a short honeymoon.

After our honeymoon, we rented a two bedroom apartment as our first home. We sought God's will for our future. I continued working for

Old Country Buffet. Tim continued his study, and worked as a security guard at Evangel.

We had a lot of things to work on during our first month of marriage. Communication has always been very important, because we came from different cultures. Misunderstandings have often occurred. But we always prayed together and learned to trust God to guide us.

By June of 1997, after six month of our marriage, I found out that I was pregnant. In a way I was happy, but I was scared, because we didn't have any savings. I was worried to death about how to take care of a child when I still acted like a child sometimes. I was 24 years old. How will I provide for my child with little money? How will I raise the baby since I didn't have any experience? I was going nuts. My parents told me to read children's storybooks more often, and think good thoughts about the baby. And listening to lots of music would help the baby grow.

During the nine months, I prayed daily for the baby to be healthy. Tim and I asked the Lord to prepare our hearts to raise the baby in a godly way. I was having morning and night sickness for four months. The ultra-sound showed my baby would be a girl. Of course, my husband wanted a boy, since he has two daughters already. My mom told me to be nice to them, and so I did.

I continued working at Old Country Buffet until the day before the baby was born. After six months, I had to reduce my working hours, and money was tight. My husband tried to help bring more money in, by picking up his old carnival glass business, which was something quite unknown to me. My manager scheduled me to work two hours a day, just to pour coffee and tea for the customers, since I was not able to do lifting toward the end of pregnancy. I had two baby showers. One was from my co-workers and the other from my church.

My baby's due date was January 31st, 1998, but she decided to surprise us. I had read books about labor pain, but I had never experienced it until 1 am, Saturday morning, January 24th. I was in pain, but I didn't know it was labor pain. I thought I must have eaten something bad, and that caused me to have stomach cramps. I told my husband that I was hurting, but he was in deep sleep and couldn't even wake up. I thought the pain would go away, but it continued for another four hours. I could not sleep and my back was hurting at the same time. I just couldn't make myself comfortable.

So, I got out of bed, and laid down on my couch in the living room. I felt relaxed, so I thought I could go back to sleep. Then, my water broke right away after I laid on the couch. I have read about how it felt when one's water broke. So I woke up my husband and told him to take me to the hospital. It was about six-in-the-morning. My husband got so excited that he ran into the bathroom. He showered and shaved. After he came out of the bathroom, he called everybody on the list which we made together, and told them that I was going to have a baby. Thank God, my pain had stopped while he was doing all of that, otherwise I would have hit him on the head. Finally, he drove me to the hospital.

It was 7 am when the hospital admitted me. After twelve hours of labor, and with the help of a C-section, I gave birth to a beautiful and healthy baby girl. Dr. Kean came to see me while I was in labor.

Leianna Elisabeth Cantrell was born at 7:55 pm, Saturday, January 24th, 1998. She weighed seven pounds, one ounce, and was nineteen and a half inches long. She was a screamer and a kicker. After the nurses cleaned her, they laid her by my side while the doctor stitched me up. I talked to her and she recognized my voice.

She wanted to look at me, but because of the bright light in the operating room, she couldn't open her eyes. So, she laid quietly until my husband took her to meet family members.

Whenever I recall the scene of the reaction of my daughter, I think of us as newborn babies to God our Father. When he calls us, we know his voice and are willing to follow him. **"My sheep hear my voice, and I know them, and they follow me"** (John 10:27).

I spent three days in the hospital. During that time, I learned to change her diaper, and started breast feeding. I had done baby-sitting before. But everything was different when it came to my own child. I was so afraid that she was going to fall out of bed when she slept by my side. I got nervous when my co-workers and friends came over to see her. I was afraid that she would catch germs or something to make her sick. My customers Bill and Louise came to see me while I was in the hospital.

We went home after three days. I learned it was not easy to take care of a newborn baby. She screamed when she was wet, she screamed when she was hungry. She kicked when she was excited. I thought that she would never stop screaming. We lived on the third floor of the complex. When my daughter screamed, the whole building could hear her. She was hungry all the time. I had to feed her every two hours, and she made me sore for quite a long time. I was nursing and bottle-feeding.

My husband did all he could to help me. He was more patient with the baby than I was. My mother-in-law and ladies from church also helped me during that time. I want to give special thanks to Estalee, my mother-in-law, who has been faithfully helping us through these years.

After my maternity leave was over, I went back to work at Old Country Buffet. My husband would bring Leianna to work to see me. I would talk to her and play with her. My daughter was content after I fed her and talked to her. All of my co-workers and customers loved her.

As she grew bigger, she became curious about everything. She crawled everywhere. Just let me say it in a simple way, she enjoyed to try her parents patience.

On my days off, I would put Leianna in a stroller and walk to the Other Mothers Store and IGA down the street. I found my daughter was fascinated by the sight-seeing. I would tell her what things were called, and she would smile as though she understood. So that had become our ritual.

I heard people talk about how a little child could sense the presence of God easier than adults. My daughter proved them right.

One day when she was one year old, she was sitting on the bed, and she said, "ABBA". When we were at church, she would suddenly stand up during the service, and wave her little hand to the empty space. I personally believed that she sensed the presence of God, and she waved to the Lord. My husband and I prayed that the Lord would draw her near to him and accept him as her Lord and Savior.

Shelly Lewis is my friend. She was my co-worker at OCB. She and her husband came to visit me at the hospital after my daughter was born. She told me she was going to have a baby too. Six month later, Shelly gave birth to Matthew Ryan Lewis. Leianna and Matthew have been good friends. They played together like brother and sister. They fight sometimes too.

My husband continued his carnival glass business. We bought a computer, so that he could buy and sell on E-Bay. He also attends Carnival Glass Conventions around the country. I hated the idea of him being away from home, and my daughter missed him so much that she would not go to sleep at night, because daddy was not there to kiss her goodnight. It was tough for us, but the Lord brought us through. He is faithful.

As I am writing this experience, I like to reflect my situation on an Old Testment story. During the reign of King Ahab, there was a terrible drought for three years. The widow and her son were about to die. So she picked up some sticks and was ready to make their last meal. God sent Elijah to see her, and asked her to fix him something to eat. She hesitated, but then obeyed, because Elijah promised that the Lord would provide her needs. After she obeyed, she never lacked any flour, and her oil jar did not run dry for three years during the drought. My experiences were similar to the widow's. Only there wasn't any drought, but finanicial difficulties. I thought that I was never able to provide enough clothing, food and toys for my daughter. And I did not like my husband's antique business. But God was faithful to us and carried us through, just like he did for that widow and her son. I had so many worries and doubts, but being willing to obey God was more important.

I thank the Lord every day for the precious gift we received from him. Leianna has been a joy to my heart. She taught me the love of God from her embrace and her smile. I just pray that she will receive the Lord and serve him.

I am thankful for God's faithfulness. His love is everlasting.

"Though the mountains be shaken and the hills be removed, yet my unfailing love for you will not be shaken nor my covenant of peace be removed," says the Lord, who has compassion on you" (Isaiah 54:10, NIV).

"Know therefore that the Lord thy God, he is God, the faithful God, which keepeth covenant and mercy with them that love him and keep his commandments to a thousand generations" (Deuteronomy 7:9).

Praise his Holy Name!

Chapter Seven

Heaven: A Place of Peace and Joy

Over the years, I have heard people praise a delicious meal as Heavenly. When I went to Florida with my family for vacation, I saw the ocean and the people relaxing on the beach, and I thought that would be an excellent picture of Heaven on earth. I have attended many funerals. It doesn't matter if they were Christians or non-Christians, I would hear the preacher say, "They are in Heaven now, and may they rest in peace". In John's Gospel, Jesus, before his betrayal, told His disciples, "My Father has so many mansions . . . I am going there to prepare a place for you" (14:2).

After I was saved, I learned that through Jesus, I could have eternal life. But I have always questioned what would Heaven be like? Would those deceased people really go to Heaven? How and where will I spend eternity? I found my answer in a tearful way.

In January of 1998, Dr. Kean visited me in the hospital when I was in labor. After my daughter was born, I was so busy taking care of Leianna, and working at the same time. Tim was going to graduate in December, so he was busy with school. We didn't find time to take Leianna to meet Dr. Kean.

In July, when Leianna was six month old, I took her to school to visit. In the hallway of the Fine Arts building, I was greeted by Dr. Kean. I could not believe how thin she was. She told me how cute my daughter looked, and then she walked away. I thought she was in a hurry, so I didn't bother to ask her how she was doing. A month later, my husband told me that Dr. Kean was very ill, and she needed prayer. I went to see Pastor Colbaugh and found out Dr. Kean suffered from lung cancer. First, she thought she had a lung infection, so she didn't give much attention to it. After she came back from Poland in August, she became very sick. She finally went to see the doctor, and they told her that she had lung cancer and was in need of treatment. While she was taking the treament, she began to have horrible headaches. Doctors explained that the cancer has gone into her brain. It was not operable.

I called Dr. Kean, and she asked me to pray for her. I did pray for healing. But I didn't realize she had become worse. At the end of October, I went to see her at Maranatha Village. I was not able to talk to her, because she was sleeping. I told her daughter-in-law, who was watching her, that I would come back to see her some other time. I didn't know that was the last time for me to see her on earth.

The morning of November 12, 1998, my husband called me from school and told me that Dr. Kean had passed away. I was shocked by the news, and regretted that I didn't even say good-bye to her. I questioned why God took this wonderful lady away? She was only sixty-five years old.

I went to her funeral at school, and listened to people share her life stories. I missed her so badly that I was getting sick. By that time, I knew I was saved, and I knew I could have eternal life, but I didn't have any knowledge about Heaven.

The thoughts about where Dr. Kean was, and how the Lord was taking care of her wore me out. I would pray a little and then I would get so angry.

One night, about two months after her passing, the Lord showed me a vision while I was asleep. In the vision, I was standing in a place where I've never been before, and I heard someone call my name. I turned around and saw Dr. Kean. She looked so healthy and happy. She passed by me with a big smile on her face, and she kept on walking. I called, "Dr. Kean, Stop!" She stopped and turned to look at me. I asked her, "Can I hug you one more time?" She agreed silently, and walked toward me. I went to meet her half way and hugged her, and we said the Lord's prayer together. I sensed my spirit and hers joined together. I was in tears when I woke up, and I praise the Lord for what he had shown me.

The Lord knew how much I cared about Dr. Kean. So, he provided the vision for me to know that Dr. Kean is indeed in his presence and she is happy. The vision was God's assurance of life eternal. What a blessing!

From that day on, I learned that my hope and joy is in Jesus. And I know that I will join Dr. Kean when my time comes.

I did not see Dr. Bussmann after my wedding. He was a busy man. I called him once in a while to tell him how I was doing. The last time I called him was on his birthday,

December 24th, 1999. And on January 14th, 2000, he had a heart attack and died at age 54. I went to his memorial service. His three children had grown up, and they remembered me. It was an emotional moment. I see Mrs. Bussmann once in a while and she is doing fine.

I didn't question where he was at that time. I knew he is resting in peace. I remember what he always said to me whenever he was ready to leave, "Peace be with you, Lei."

However, I did question why the Lord would take these precious people at such a young age. And the Word of God revealed his answer to me in this way: **"So is my words that goes out from my mouth: It will not return to me empty, but will accomplish what I desire and achieve the purpose for which I send it" (Isaiah 55:11, NIV).**

"And God shall wipe away all tears from their eyes; and there shall be no more death, neither sorrow, nor crying, neither shall there be any more pain; for the former things are passed away" (Revelation 21:4).

"For my Father's Will is that everyone who looks to the Son and believes in Him shall have eternal life, and I will raise him up at the last day" (John 6:40, NIV).

Dr. Kean and Dr. Bussmann accomplished what God desired of them. Their lives were full and successful. It is certainly not easy to let them go. But to know they are in our Heavenly Father's care fills our hearts with comfort and peace. Thank you Jesus for your death and resurrection, so that I could have hope and faith in you. I praise your name, Amen! and Amen!

Chapter Eight

Old Country Buffet: The Training Ground

I have mentioned Old Country Buffet so many times in the last few chapters. Now, I think it is time to write about it.

I started working there in September of 1996. The restaurant was operated by a General Manager who is the boss of kitchen and service managers. There is a service supervisor who assists those managers and employees on the food line, and servers who take care of customers in the dining room.

I have been with this company for over seven years. For the first five years, I worked mainly as a dining room attendant, and as a line server once in a while. As a dining room attendant, I had a strict supervisor. Her name was Gwen. She was easy to talk to when she was not on duty. Once she started working, it would be very hard to catch her, because she walks so fast. She wanted everything to be done perfectly, and of course in the Buffet way. She could be really pushy and bossy sometimes, and made me really want to walk out the door and never return. But I decided to stay. I believed that a good supervisor could train up a good employee.

I certainly didn't consider myself a good employee, because it seemed I was the only frequent visitor to my manager's office. I would always get disciplined by Ms. Sissy Kahl, the general manager. She would tell me what I did wrong and expected me to do a better job. So, I would try hard to work on the things which she told me to make improvement.

Ms. Kahl is an easy-going person. You can talk to her about sports and things in your life, when she is not upset or under pressure. She tries hard to treat every employee equally. But, when she is angry, watch out and be quiet and do whatever she says!

So many times, I got frustrated after I was called to the office to be scolded by Sissy. I would fuss at the Lord, and questioned God on why he wants me to work there. I have had doubts and anxieties during the time at OCB. For a little while, besides working and making money, and then coming home to complain how tired I was, I couldn't figure out what was God's purpose for me to work there. Then when I saw how my customers enjoyed to hear my life story, and I found opportunities to tell some of my co-workers about the Lord and what he has done in my life, I realized that the Lord put me there to do his work.

I was promoted to be a supervisor in 2001, and I found myself easily getting irritated by the customers and my co-workers. But whenever I was under pressure or frustrated, Sissy would teach me to take a deep breath, put a smile on my face and go back to work. Ms. Kahl understood my frustration. Her encouragement and trust has strengthed me to continue my job as supervisor. I have learned a lot from her during these years.

I have thought about her teaching and discipline to me as the way the Lord does to his children. When we are tired and weary, he would strengthen us with his words. When we are going astray, he is there to discipline us. So, I thank Sissy for godly counsel without knowing it. And may the Lord bless her.

So, I will continue to work there, and to serve my customers and be friends with my co-workers. And I pray for the company and my managers that the blessings of the Lord will be upon them. May the Lord increase the business and make it prosper continually.

"That every man should eat and drink, and enjoy the good of all his labour -- it is the gift of God" (Ecclesiastes 3:13).

Chapter Nine

May the Peace of God Rule in Your Heart Because He Is The Peace

I have been thinking about this subject for a long time, and now I believe it is a perfect time to write about it. I want to dedicate this writing to the Lord's Resurrection. But first let me pray: Lord, I have been blessed by your grace and mercy, and I like to share my testimony with others, to encourage them to be a blessing to one another, and to thank you for what you have done in our lives. Most of all, to believe that you are always there for us. I want to glorify your Holy Name. In Jesus name I pray, Amen!

In the Spring of 1996, I was dating the person who is now my husband. I came from a different culture and was burdened by his past. I remember I was stressed out, depressed, and not able to do anything. My heart was very heavy. I didn't know who to turn to, and it looked like everyone and everything in the world was against me. I felt like crying and screaming: I was torn within. But the turning point came after all of the depression. One afternoon, after class, I lay down on my bed and poured out my heart to my Heavenly Father. My prayer was: "Lord, I don't know what to do, and I can't handle this anymore. I have to give everything to you. If it is your will for me to date this person, may your will be done." I wasn't quite finished praying, but I felt something moving the burden which was as heavy as a mountain out of my heart. And I felt great peace and joy come into my heart instead. I have not a clue how my emotion changed so instantly. I was able to rest a little, but my spirit was rejoicing for the peace I was given. When my boyfriend called me, he was extrememly happy to hear me giggle. **"Till he fill thy mouth with laughing, and thy lips with rejoicing" (Job 8:21).** I realized it was the Lord who heard my prayer and moved my burden away. Because he has said: **"Peace I leave with you; my peace I give unto you: not as the world giveth, give I unto you. Let not your heart be troubled, neither let it be afraid" (John 14:27).**

And now, Tim and I have been married over seven year. We have our ups and downs, but we thank God each day that he brought us together.

"Cast all your care upon him, for he careth for you" (1 Peter 5:7).

We are human, and when we are troubled, it is very easy to say, "Oh, what am I going to do?" or "Oh, this is terrible!" I admit that I fit in that picture, and I am struggling with it daily.

I prayed for my parents to come to visit for a long time, and the Lord answered that prayer. But the result was a big mess. I blamed my husband for not being sensitive to my needs. I blamed myself for not listening to my parents and marrying my husband. I was like a three-year-old, and kept questioning why this mess was happening. But one thing I didn't do: I didn't ask the Lord. After my parents went home, I sought the Lord. And I realized that whatever happened during my parents visit was not a surprise to the Lord. He set this big test for me to see how much I can rely on him. He was waiting for me to put trust and faith in him. Because **"God is our refuge and strength,** a very present help in trouble. Therefore will not we fear, though the earth be removed, and though the mountains be carried into the midst of the sea" (Psalms 46:1,2). After I thought it through, I knew that I should depend on him and trust him more in times of trouble. We as humans easily change, but our Heavenly Father will not change. He is always there, and because he loves us and cares for us, we can trust him and he gives peace. Just like the verse in the song "Wonderful Peace"says:"Ah! soul, are you here without comfort or rest . . . make Jesus your friend . . . O accept this sweet peace so sublime! Peace! Peace! wonderful peace, coming down from Father above!" Whenever I sing this song, it reminds me of his nearness and care for me. Praise God Almighty. He is wonderful!

Tuesday, September 11, 2001 was the day that no one could forget. From my point of view, it was a time that brought me much closer to the Lord. That morning, my husband left at 5:00 am for a business meeting in Kansas City. I just wanted to go back to sleep. Around 5:30 or 6:00 am, I felt warmness coming upon me, and there were two voices whispering in my ear, saying "Jesus! Jesus! Jesus!" in English and

"The Kingdom of God" in Chinese. They kept repeating themselves. They were so close and intense, it made me a little scared. Meanwhile, I saw a wall with soft light on it. Even though I knew instantly that I was in the presence of God, I had no clue why everything was so intense, until four hours later I tried to watch the weather report. There was no weather and no TV shows, except the terrible Live report on the tragedy of the Twin Towers.

First, I didn't relate my experience with the news at all. But after I talked to my pastor and shared my experience with other Christians, they told me similar stories. I understood God was trying to assure me that as his child, I should not be afraid of what was happening, but have faith in him. Because it is written: **"There shall no evil befall thee, neither shall any plague come nigh thy dwelling. For he shall give his angels charge over thee, to keep thee in all thy ways" (Psalms 91:10,11).** And also rejoice even in times such as this. Isaiah said:**"For ye shall go out with joy and be led forth with peace" (Isaiah 55:12).** Praise God, for he is wonderful, his love will never fail, his mercy is upon those who love and trust him. The song comes to my mind, "Turn your eyes upon Jesus; look full in his wonderful face, And the things of earth will grow strangly dim in the light of his glory and grace." Glory to God in the Highest! HalleluYah!

God is joy, his love and mercy shall not end. God is the peace, and **"Now the Lord of peace himself give you peace always by all means. The Lord be with you all" (2 Thessalonians 3:16). "And let the peace of God rule in your hearts, to the which also ye are called in one body; and be ye thankful" (Colossians 3:15).**

Chapter Ten

Unlimited Mercy of God

The story of Jonah has been a good example for people to learn the lessons of repentance and forgiveness. The story which I am going to tell shows the fruit of forgiveness and God's mercy beyond human measure.

My friend Shelly's son Matthew and my daughter Leianna are growing up together. They are good friends.

One day, Shelly and I had an argument over our children. It started when they came to visit us. My daughter and Matthew were fighting over a video tape. Matthew got so upset that he hit Leianna. Leianna started to cry and I was shocked and angry, so I yelled at Matthew at the top of my lungs. Shelly calmed me down by telling Matthew to apologize to Leianna. And then she said, "I see kids hit each other on the playground all the time." I couldn't believe what I heard. But I thought as long as I keep Leianna away from Matthew, it would be all right. My husband wasn't happy that Leianna got hit, and he told me to tell Shelly that not only should Matthew not hit Leianna, but that he should not hit anybody, especially girls.

I thought that Shelly as an adult should understand it. So, I didn't even bother to talk to her. I felt uncomfortable with Shelly and Matthew around. I asked the Lord to help me to be patient with them.

We were doing well for a little while. But one day, when the four of us came back from the library, Matthew was upset. He wanted something from the library, but it was not there. So, he started crying and fussing. I prayed in my heart that we would get home quickly.

Well, Shelly explained to Matthew that he would certainly get what he wanted at the next trip to the library. That child wouldn't budge, and fussed even more. He kicked and kicked and made Shelly extremely frustrated. She threatened if he didn't stop, he would be spanked. By the time we pulled into my driveway, Matthew had nowhere to shed his temper, so he hit Leianna again.

At that moment, I'd had enough. I jumped out of the car and tried to get Leianna to stop crying. Shelly was upset and spanked Matthew and made him apologize to my daughter. After

I got Leianna in the house, I told my husband what had happened. I was so angry that I couldn't talk clearly.

After I cooled off a little bit, I went out to check on Shelly and Matthew. I didn't want to talk about the problem, all I wanted to do was to make sure Shelly and Matthew were all right, because I knew Matthew had apologized to my daughter. But to my amazement, Shelly began to blame me for overreacting, and for not accepting her child's behavior as common and normal. Again, she said that she has seen similar behavior on the playground. I became so angry, I could hardly talk. So, I went back to my house and Shelly and Matthew went home.

That night before I went to bed, I cried out to the Lord. I asked the Lord to show me His will. I asked the Lord to forgive me for being so angry, and to protect my daughter wherever she goes. Then, the Lord showed me in a vision that my friendship with Shelly will be much closer than ever.

I told my husband to e-mail Shelly, and to tell her how to resolve the conflict. My husband was upset by the fact that our daughter has been hit a second time. His message was simply to tell Shelly and her husband that they should find a suitable way to train Matthew to be a gentleman, and for him to learn that he should not hit anybody, especially girls. Shelly's response was that her son had been disciplined. My anger went out of control.

Although I remembered the Lord's promise about our friendship, I could not picture myself being friends with that woman. I found myself depressed, and I was irritated by the Word of the Lord on forgiving. Shelly called and talked to me about how she felt. The phone call didn't get rid of my anger, but only made it worse. I wondered why God would want to have mercy on this kind of people. I asked the Lord to show me some other solution, so I didn't have to deal with her any more. But He was silent.

You know, the prophet Jonah didn't want to obey God's command, and was swallowed by the big fish, and he stayed in the belly of the big fish for three days. After Jonah earnestly prayed, God delivered him.

I certainly didn't get swallowed by the fish, but I felt like I'd been swallowed by the darkness. The more I thought about breaking up the friendship with Shelly, the more I stayed in the darkness, and it lasted for two weeks.

On the third week, I poured out my heart to the Lord, and asked him to deliver me out of the darkness. His answer was very simple, "Do what I have told you to do, and you and Shelly will be much closer than ever." I prayed the Lord would guide my thoughts to know how to speak to Shelly.

Finally, Shelly and I sat down and talked. She stated that she was angry and tried to protect her son. So she didn't want to hear what I had to say. She then apologized for being stubborn. She asked me to talk to her right away about any problem we might have in the future. And she would understand if I didn't want to continue our friendship.

I told her how I felt. And I told her about God's promise for our friendship. I agreed with her about solving problems right away. As we both forgave each other, the presence of God filled the room. It was a marvelous feeling.

At the end we prayed together, and asked God's blessing on our friendship. It has been over a year since that incident. We have been closer than ever, just as the Lord promised.

From my experience, I learned that God is sovereign and in control. It is hard to submit to his perfect will sometimes, but he knows best. And his mercy has no measure. The Lord has declared this in his words:

"But the mercy of the Lord is from everlasting to everlasting upon them that fear him, and his righteousness unto children's children" (Psalms 103:17).

"And he said, "I will make all my goodness to pass before thee, and I will proclaim the name of the Lord before thee; and will be gracious to whom I will be gracious, and will show mercy on whom I will show mercy" (Exodus 33:19).

I give thanks and glory to His Holy Name.

Chapter Eleven

"Stand Still, and See the Salvation of God"
(Exodus 14:13)

Dear Lord, as I am writing this testimony, I like for people to learn more about you and the amazing work that you are doing. As you are trying to bring more people into your Kingdom, we as your children will stand still and see your Salvation and glory. I pray that people will come to you and seek your face to follow you. Because **"For this is good, and acceptable in the sight of God our Saviour; Who wants all men to be saved and to come unto a knowledge of the truth"** (1 Timothy 2: 3,4). Also, I like to use this testimony to encourage oversea missionaries to have joy and faith in him and glorify his Holy Name.

The voice of rejoicing and salvation is in the tabernacles of the righteous: the right hand of the Lord doeth valiantly" (Psalms 118:15)!

I have been overwhelmed with the mighty work he has done recently. It began a month ago on a Sunday afternoon, while I was at work. I sat down with my Bulgarian and Latino co-workers for lunch. Soon I found myself involved in a conversation about marriage and adultery. The Bulgarian guy stated that not all of the married couples in his country stay faithful to each other. And he asked me if I have any boyfriends, even though he knew I am married. I told him no. But he didn't believe me, and said that I was drunk and not telling him the truth. So, I said that God would strike me down if I did adultery. But the more I stayed on my biblical ground, the more he laughed and mocked me. After he went back to work, I sat there and laughed for his ignorance, but my heart was burdened for him. I went to church that night and asked everybody to pray for him. I was thinking maybe I needed to find some translators to help me with this matter.

About two days later while I was working, a couple from Finland was dining in the restaurant. I found out that they are Christians and work for Patmos Foundation for World Missions. So, I asked them if they happen to know of any Bulgarian Bibles or tracts. They said they might and recorded my name and address. They also gave me their business cards.

A month later, I received a package in the mail. I was shocked because my husband is usually the only one who receives packages for his antique business. Inside this special package were three books in a foreign language which I could not read nor understand. As I was trying to figure out what they were, my 5-year-old daughter said "Bible," because she saw the cross on the book cover. The light bulb went on and I realized that they are Bulgarian Bibles. Also enclosed was a letter in English, which read:

> *"Dear Lei,*
> *You have met our president, and mission doctor at the restaurant. They told me that there are a few young men in your restaurant who need the Gospel in Bulgarian. They asked me to send you 'some tools' . . . so you find two New Testaments and one Bible in Bulgarian."*

I could not express my feelings. First, I was too shocked to talk, and then I was so excited. I knew the Lord has answered my prayer in an amazing way beyond my expectation. I e-mailed the lady who sent the Bible to thank her. At church that night, I asked everyone to pray that my co-workers will seek the Lord once I gave them the Bibles.

Humanly speaking, I believed the Lord answered my prayer by sending the Bibles. But you know the Lord has a sense of humor. He will accomplish his work by his desire in his timing. And there was more to come in God's own plan.

Sunday, before I went to work, I picked out some Scriptures on Salvation, God's judgement on adultery, and our body as the Temple of God. I thought God will use these Scriptures to speak to them. Then I took the Bibles to work. I feared for the worst reaction my co-worker would give me.

When I handed the New Testament and Bible to the Bulgarian co-worker, his eyes turned red, and he could not put down the Bible. He was so excited that he kept saying, "Bulgarian, Bulgarian language!" After they have scanned the Bible and New Testament, they explained to me in broken English, "Old and new." I realized these books were written in Old Bulgarian and new Bulgarian version. It is like King James version and New International version. I was speechless after they told me in broken English:" Tonight, no friends, no drinking, no dancing, go home, read Bible."

All I knew to say was, "Good for you." But my heart was overwhelmingly rejoicing over the mighty work of God. I sensed his Presence in that place more than ever. I wanted to jump up and down. The Scripture said: **"The Lord thy God in the midst of thee is mighty; he will save, he will rejoice over thee with joy; he will rest in his love, he will joy over thee with singing" (Zephania 3:17).** Isaiah stated: **"O Lord, thou art my God; I will exalt thee, and praise thy name; for thou has done wonderful things; thy counsels of old are faithfulness and truth" (Isaiah 25:1).** Praise God, HalleluYah!

After all this excitment, you may ask what did I do with the Scriptures I had picked out for them. Well, I did nothing, because it wasn't God's timing. I was completely speechless and in awe of how marvelous our God is.

As I am pondering on this event, I like to reflect on the children of Israel, when God led them out of Egypt. They were facing the Red Sea, with Egyptian army behind them. They complained and feared for the attack of the army. They could not remember it was the Lord God Almighty who brought them out. And yet God was not going to leave them there. He wanted them to see his full Glory. Moses said: "Fear not, stand still, and see the salvation of the Lord" (Exodus 14:13). I don't know what those people were thinking, but I can imagine that they were quite amazed with the departing and closing of the Red Sea -- how the Lord God defeated the Egyptians, and all the people of Israel had to do was to be obedient and follow God's command and trust his mighty power. As for myself with my own experience, I know I have seen his Glory, and was speechless and in awe as I have written earlier. **"For all the promises of God in him are yea, and in him Amen, unto the glory of God by us" (2 Corinthians 1:20).**

"Trust in the Lord with all thy heart and lean not on your own understanding; In all thy ways acknowledge him, and he will direct thy paths" (Proverbs 3: 5,6).

I learned a precious lesson from my experience. God works in his way, and his timing. **"So shall my Word be that goes forth out of my mouth: It will not return unto me void, but it shall accomplish that which I please, and it shall prosper in the thing whereto I send it" (Isaiah 55:11).** He uses us as his messengers. Sometimes we like to work in our own way, even though we might do it in the name of the Lord. But he is the mighty one, from whom we seek strength and comfort.

When we face our daily duties or problems, it doesn't matter big or small, we like to try to figure it out by ourselves in our way. When we fail, we like to complain and whine. That is why we should remember God is the one who is in control of our lives. His love for us is beyond measure. He never fails us.

In closing, I like to remind you that God is working in his way and timing, and he will show you the mighty things. And we are going to **"Stand still and see the Salvation of God."** Praise His Holy Name. Amen! Amen!

My Final Thoughts

For an atheist, if you happen to read my experiences: I want you to know that God does exist. He is waiting for you to turn to him and find the true meaning of life.

For a new believer, and you are standing at the crossroad: I want you to know that you have renewed yourself in him. Be joyful, but cautious, because you have just walked out of the darkness, and Satan does not like to be losing you. Therefore, you must follow closely to the Word of God. Seek his face, and he will reveal himself to you.

For those of you who have been with him and have experienced his love, mercy and power: I am glad that I can share my testimony with you.

For those of you who have walked away from him: I want you to know that he still loves you and waits patiently for your return.

For those of you who are foreigners: I want you to know that God may use you mightily to bring the lost ones to his Kingdom.

I thank the Lord for he has given me this opportunity to share my stories with you. As humans, we all have had happiness and struggles with life. But God is faithful toward his servants.

I want you to know that God is love, his mercy has no measure, and he is with us. May "God Is With Us" -- the song the Lord has given me -- encourage everyone, that he is indeed caring for us:

God Is With Us

God is with us, God is with us
Through temptation, trials, and tears
God is with us, God is with us
He is with us through the years.

God is with us, God is with us
Through His Spirit from above
God is with us, God is with us
Bringing Peace and Joy and Love.

God is with us, God is with us
Even when our anger flares
God is with us, God is with us
Overcoming Satan's snares.

God is with us, God is with us
Showing us Emmanuel
God is with us, God is with us
Sending us, the world to tell.

God is with us, God is with us
Listening to all our prayers
God is with us, God is with us
Teaching us that JESUS CARES.

God is with us, God is with us
Sending Jesus to amend
God is with us, God is with us
He'll be with us to the end.

In closing, I want to say the last ten years were what I call the foundation of my relationship with God. As I begin each new chapter of my life, I believe that he has wonderful things in store for me. Just like a little child is so eager to unwrap the Christmas gifts, I can't wait to unwrap mine.

Made in the USA
San Bernardino, CA
15 January 2018